2003-2004 NMI
MISSION EDUCATION RESOURCES

❊ ❊ ❊

READING BOOKS

THE FAR SIDE OF THE SEA
From the Philippines to Ukraine
by Lynn DiDominicis

FLOODS OF COMPASSION*
Hope for Honduras
by Paul Jetter

IMPACT!*
Work and Witness Miracles
by J. Wesley Eby

THE JAGGED EDGE OF SOMEWHERE*
by Amy Crofford

THE LAND OF THE LONG WHITE CLOUD
Nazarenes in New Zealand
by Connie Griffith Patrick

SECOND WIND
Running the Race in Retirement
by Sherry Pinson

*Youth Books

❊ ❊ ❊

ADULT MISSION EDUCATION RESOURCE BOOK

CALLED TO GO
Edited by Wes Eby

IMPACT

Work & Witness Miracles

by J. Wesley Eby

Nazarene Publishing House
Kansas City, Missouri

10   9   8   7   6   5   4   3   2   1

Dedicated to each person—
thousands upon thousands—
who has ever participated
in a Work and Witness experience.
Your impact on missions worldwide,
as well as the trip's impact on you personally,
is eternal.

Pronunciation Guide

Aymara	ie-MAH-rah
Banmai Patana	BAHN-mie pah-tah-NAH
Cesar	SAY-zahr
Champs Elysées	SHAHM see-lee-SAY
Changuinola	chahng-gee-NOH-lah
Cliza	KLEE-sah
Cochabamba	koh-chah-BAHM-bah
Eglise du Nazareen	ay-GLEEZ doo naz-uh-REEN
El Esfuerzo	EHL ehs-FWAYR-soh
Farag	FAYR-ihg
Feliciano Sep	fay-lee-see-AHN-oh SEHP
Guayaquil	GWIE-uh-KEEL
Jasuh Jana	jah-SUH jah-NAH
Kesorn	kay-SOHRN
Lahu	LAH-hoo
Myanmar	MEE-ahn-mah
Nanthawat Jantib	NAHN-tah-WAHT jahn-TEEB
Ojo de Agua	OH-hoh day AH-gwah
Paquito Bido	pah-KEE-toh BEE-doh
Paso Grande	PAH-soh GRAHN-day
Pokomchí	poh-kohm-CHEE
quetzales	kayt-SAH-lays
Quito	KEE-toh
Reyzie	RAY-zee
Saenz	SIENZ
Tecush comen	tay-KOOSH koh-MEHN
Yangmi	YAHNG-me

Contents

J. Wesley Eby is mission education coordinator for Nazarene Missions International (NMI) for the Church of the Nazarene, assuming this role in 1998. In this capacity he serves as editor for the NMI reading book program and Adult Mission Education (AME) curriculum.

Wes, as he is best known, has been employed at Headquarters for 16 years, previously working as an ESL (English as a second language) editor in Publications International (now World Mission Literature) for 9 years and as managing editor of *Herald of Holiness* (now *Holiness Today*) for 2 years.

Before moving to Kansas City, he spent 29 years in the education field, of which 22 years were on the Navajo Reservation as a teacher, administrator, and ESL specialist. Growing up in a Nazarene parsonage, Wes was surrounded by family members who were ministers and missionaries. His heritage, education, and work experience have made a major impact on his life, especially for missions.

As a writer, Wes coauthored an NMI reading book, *Wherever God Plants Us,* with his stepmother and former missionary, Dorothy Bevill Eby. He has written numerous articles for church publications as well as ESL materials, including *Handbook for Teaching Bible-Based ESL.* He is coauthor of the *Dictionary of the Bible and Christian Doctrine in Everyday English.*

Wes and his wife, Roberta, have four married sons—Edward, Joseph, Robert, and Daniel—and six grandchildren. He and his wife are members of the Overland Park, Kansas, Church of the Nazarene.

Foreword

How blessed I was. . . . It gave me a heart for missions. . . . I really needed that firsthand experience. . . . I have to do something, for the need is so great. . . . I had to see for myself. . . . I was filled with a deep sense of accomplishment. . . . I was changed.

These are some of the statements you will read throughout this book. And I have heard similar statements, over and over and over again, as I talk to Work and Witness (W&W) participants.

Through this get-involved-and-get-your-hands-dirty ministry, hundreds of thousands have been impacted.

Without question, Work and Witness is one of the greatest lay movements, past or present, in the Church of the Nazarene. This missions ministry brings people together from various countries and cultures, working shoulder-to-shoulder, to impact the Kingdom—and miracles result.

I'm always amazed—but I shouldn't be, I know —to learn what God is doing in and through the lives of those who are obedient to the Work and Witness call—a call to service, sacrifice, and selflessness. Through this get-involved-and-get-your-hands-dirty ministry, hundreds of thousands have been impacted. And while those who become involved give generously of their time, skills, energy, and resources, they are the ones who testify to receiving the most blessings.

Who can begin to calculate the investment that has been made around the world through W&W? The number of buildings that teams have erected, restored, and renovated is countless and impossible even to estimate. But W&W is far more than new buildings, donated money, and overseas trips. Lives have been, are being, and will be changed—eternally!

I'm confident you'll enjoy reading these short, impact-filled stories. If you've been on a Work and Witness team, you'll find yourself recalling the adventure and remembering all God did to make it possible. If you haven't, I hope you'll be challenged to experience W&W for yourself. It will change you forever. Guaranteed!

—Marty Hoskins
Director of Candidate Development and Volunteerism
World Mission Division

Acknowledgments

A book of this nature would be impossible without the contributions of many people. I'm deeply indebted to the individuals who shared their stories, leaving a forever impact on my mind and heart:

Marty Hoskins
Larry Webb
David Hane
Roxanne Alexander
Alex Mahaffey
Gary Hasenauer
Jeff Croft
Marvin McLain
Karen Robbins

I'm grateful for the numerous volunteers mentioned in this book, who have given selflessly of themselves to become involved in missions around the world through Work and Witness.

I wish to thank all those who have assisted me in bringing these stories to the printed page:

- Gail Sawrie, Nazarene Missions International (NMI) colleague, for her wise counsel and editing skills.
- My dedicated NMI office coworkers—Nina Gunter, Karen Jones, Linda Phelps, Melinda Miller, Shirley Bortner, and Jo Doerr—for their encouragement and go-for-it spirit.
- The gifted personnel at Beacon Hill Press and Nazarene Publishing House, especially Bonnie

Perry, Paul Martin, Royce Ratcliff, Janice Sarver, Mike Walsh, and Sharon Page, for their ongoing advice and artistic touch on this book.

- The Mission Education Committee members for their confidence and commissioning me to report just a minute part of the tremendous impact of the Work and Witness ministry.
- My wife, Roberta, for reading the manuscript and giving it her loving critique, and my aunt Gladys, for her inspiration and helping to instill in me a passion for missions.
- Most of all, God the Creator, who has ordained and graced my life, allowing me to use the gift of writing for His glory.

—Wes Eby

Introduction

"Work and Witness, without question, has made the greatest impact on hands-on mission involvement of any program in the Church of the Nazarene," says Nina Gunter, general NMI director. "This dynamic ministry began as the result of a historic election in 1972 when Paul Gamertsfelder and Morris Weigelt were the first men elected to the General NMI (then NWMS) Council. Among Dr. Gamertsfelder's assignments was getting men involved in the NMI. And the rest is now history."

Dr. Paul, as he is called, after praying and thinking about this new challenge, presented his plans for Men in Missions (MIM) to key personnel in Kansas City. Mary Scott, then general NMI director, and Jerald Johnson, then director of the World Mission Department, gave their support to this new movement. And the General NMI Council gave the idea its hearty endorsement.

The first "official" Men in Missions trip took place in January 1974 in Central America. Dr. Paul and two lay couples from Ohio, who paid their own expenses, held evangelistic meetings among two indigenous Indian tribes in Panama. On this trip the dire need for adequate buildings—churches, parsonages, missionary homes—became obvious, and immediately Dr. Paul began to promote the idea of constructing buildings on the mission field.

Within the next couple of years, several Men in

Missions teams traveled to Mexico, Central America, and the Caribbean. While the countries just south of the United States were attractive due to their close proximity to the States and cheaper travel costs, soon MIM teams were making trips to other world areas—even to "the ends of the earth."

As MIM trips grew in popularity and churches contacted Dr. Paul for information, the need for a coordinator in World Mission became apparent. Rich Gammill, an employee in the missions department, was assigned to devote part-time to this ministry. When Gammill left Headquarters in 1979, James Hudson, another member of the missions staff, was asked to add MIM to his duties. In the early 1980s MIM involvement escalated to the point that a full-time coordinator was needed. David Hayse, who had been coordinating team efforts in Mexico and beyond, moved to Kansas City to accept this important responsibility. Hayse provided solid leadership for MIM/W&W for more than a decade until Marty Hoskins assumed this strategic role in 1996.

Truly, every changed life, every person who has been impacted by the W&W experience, is a miracle.

From the beginning, women were involved in Men in Missions, which included Dr. Paul's first trip to Panama. Most teams had a few females, who supported the team by preparing meals, laundering clothes, and doing the tasks many men preferred to avoid. However, some ladies labored competently at construction sites, wielding hammers, trowels, screwdrivers, and paintbrushes along-side their male counterparts. To recognize this fact and to encourage greater involvement by women, the General NMI Council officially changed the title "Men in Missions" to "Work and Witness" in 1984.

"Work and Witness and Alabaster have become inseparable companions," says Dr. Gunter. "The monies generated by both these ministries work in concert to accomplish far more than either one can by itself. Alabaster often purchases the land upon which a Work and Witness team will build a chapel or clinic or school. What a blessing this 'mission marriage' has been! And what a thrill it has been for NMI to partner with World Mission in promoting both of these vital ministries."

The cumulative record of Work and Witness (W&W) speaks for itself. Consider these remark-able—if not unbelievable—facts. As of June 30, 2002, there have been

✓7,021 teams

✓117,519 participants

✓8,724,993 donated labor hours

✓4,391 donated labor years

These significant numbers indicate that in the 29-year history of W&W there has been an average of 242 teams with 4,052 participants annually. In the almost three decades there has been an average of 4½ teams each week with a total of 78 persons ministering somewhere on planet Earth. What an impressive record! What grace-filled miracles! Truly, every changed life, every person who has been im-pacted by the W&W experience, is a miracle.

With more than 100,000 participants, there are 100,000 stories. The Work and Witness experience has impacted each individual who has taken part in specific, incredible, life-changing ways. Countless untold stories, if told, would certainly be heart-warming and awe-inspiring.

The 10 accounts in this book only represent the myriad stories embodied in the lives of every W&W participant. As you journey around the world with the people in this book, permit their stories to touch you just as the Work and Witness experience has impacted their lives.

A Life-Changing Experience

"Hey, Marty, how 'bout being a sponsor on our youth Work and Witness trip to Ecuador?" Herb asked. "I know you'll love it. Give it some serious thought."

"OK, get me the particulars," 23-year-old Marty responded rather nonchalantly.

Marty Hoskins knew the youth group had been planning this excursion for some time, but he really had no interest in participating. Even though raised in a Nazarene parsonage, he had been a Christian for just a year. Plus, he liked his job and enjoyed the Florida Gulf Coast lifestyle. A missions experience to another country held no attraction to him.

But something about Herb's invitation lodged in Marty's mind and heart. He couldn't get rid of it. Taking Herb's challenge seriously, he *did* give the trip to South America "some serious" consideration. *Hmm, it does sound interesting*, he thought. *Maybe I would enjoy it*. He could get time off from work, he had skills that would be an asset for such a project, and he was single. *There's no reason not to go*, he concluded. *I'll do it*.

"Sign me up. I'm ready to go," he told Herb

McMillan, the youth pastor at Bradenton First Church of the Nazarene, the next time the two ran into each other at church.

Eight weeks later in August 1985 Marty flew southward for a 10-day adventure, thinking it would be a wonderful experience to minister to Ecuadoreans. First, the dozen or so youth and their sponsors spent a couple of days at the regional office in Quito painting and cleaning. Then they traveled to various churches, witnessing through music and drama.

"From the first day I felt God had sent me to Ecuador for a special reason," Marty says. "As we traveled through the breathtaking Andes Mountains to hold evangelistic services, the reason—the Lord's reason—began to unfold."

Craig Zickefoose, then missionary to Ecuador, was the bus driver for the team. He shared his own story of how God had called him into missions through Work and Witness, and how he and his wife, Gail, had quit their jobs to serve as missionaries. Craig's testimony impacted Marty. "By the time we reached the coastal city of Guayaquil and the end of the trip," he says, "I was ready to rush back to Florida, quit my job, sell my car, cut all ties, and offer myself for missions."

Before leaving Ecuador, Marty talked with Louie Bustle, the director of the South America Region at that time, sharing how he felt God was leading him to volunteer on the mission field. Dr. Bustle's advice was, "Go home, pray about it, and come back on a construction project. Just make certain this is what God wants for your life."

During the following weeks, the "mission" desire was so strong that it consumed Marty's life. "I thought missions. I talked missions. I prayed missions. I planned missions. I ate and drank missions. In fact, my friends got tired of my missions enthusiasm. But I had no peace. Returning to the mission field was the only option for me."

In the meantime, his new missionary friends in Ecuador, the Zickefooses, had been transferred to Haiti. Knowing he had two weeks of vacation at Christmas, Marty contacted Craig and inquired about visiting them over the holidays. Craig immediately responded, "Come on down. We'd love to have you. In fact, we're having a Work and Witness team here during that time."

In late December Marty flew to Haiti to visit Craig and Gail and to help with building a church in a remote area. "We slept in tents on foam mats and bathed in the muddy river," Marty says. "Though it was rough, *really* rough, just seeing the church building rise from Haitian soil and observing the joy it brought to our Caribbean Nazarenes confirmed God's call to me for missions. I promised the Lord I would serve Him anywhere He would choose to lead me."

As soon as Marty returned home from the Caribbean, he contacted Louie Bustle again. "I'm ready. When can I go?"

"I'll be at your church in June," Louie answered. "Let's talk then."

The days and weeks and months seemed an eternity to Marty. The long wait was a burden. But he admits that he needed that time. "I'd been a Christian only a short while and had some maturing to do," Marty confesses. "In addition, I had a checklist of things to do before I could embark on a missions career."

When June arrived, Marty had the long-awaited, long-anticipated talk with Dr. Bustle. "We really can use you in Ecuador," Louie said. "How soon can you be ready?"

For Marty it wouldn't take long; after all, he'd been ready since the previous August. Yet, he needed some miracles. He still had some unchecked items on his list, such as selling his car. Without telling anyone, he committed each item, including the unsold vehicle, to God. One day when sitting on his car's hood, a church member drove by. The man stopped, backed up, got out, and approached Marty. "Would you sell me your car?" he said. "I want to buy it for our daughter."

As an "unattached" male, Mr. Hoskins was usually introduced to visiting teams as Marty-the-single-volunteer-who-is-looking-for-a-wife missionary.

"Just like that," Marty says, a large smile lighting his countenance, "God took care of my checklist. He handled every single detail for me, one small miracle after another."

In August 1986 the eager "missionary" headed for Quito as a Nazarene in Volunteer Service (NIVS). For the next year he joyfully helped with various construction projects and numerous work teams that traveled to Ecuador. Marty was content—ecstatically content.

Marty, a bachelor missionary

As an "unattached" male, Mr. Hoskins was usually introduced to visiting teams as Marty-the-single-volunteer-who-is-looking-for-a-wife missionary. Several well-meaning friends, attempting to play Cupid, all failed, as Cupid had plans of his own.

One year after Marty arrived on the field, a team from Santa Ana, California, came to Ecuador, and one particular team member grabbed Marty's attention immediately. Cupid's arrows hit their intended mark—Marty and Debbie—and two smitten hearts fell in love. Courtship, entirely from a distance, was brief. Engagement came in just 60 days with a wedding 6 months later. "As crazy as this sounds," Marty says, "we knew that God brought us together. We both had a strong desire and call to serve Him on the mission field."

One month after their wedding in 1988, Marty and Debbie returned to South America as volunteers (NIVS) to serve as Work and Witness coordinators. "What a marvelous privilege I had to work with the

Debbie, Marty's Work and Witness partner

22

Debbie and Marty with Caleb in Venezuela, 1995

many teams that donated their time and money and energy," Marty says.

The next few years brought several significant events and changes in the Hoskinses' lives. One year later they were granted specialized missionary status. ("Official" missionaries at last.) God called Marty to preach in 1991. (One of God's surprises.) Caleb arrived to bless their home in 1992. (The blond-haired, blue-eyed lad stood out among his Ecuadorean playmates.)

At the request of World Mission they transferred to Venezuela in 1993 and were given career missionary assignments. Marty was thrilled, as his good friend Craig Zickefoose was now the Work and Witness coordinator in the same country. He looked forward to his new challenge as administrator for the Venezuelan Field.

But the Work and Witness impact for Marty was a long way from over. Dr. Louie Bustle, now the director of the World Mission Department, invited Marty to join the mission team at the Church of the Nazarene Headquarters in Kansas City. Five months later Marty accepted the position of Work and Witness coordinator for the denomination.

"We packed our belongings and headed back to the States in April 1996," Marty says. "It was quite a change after living almost 10 years in South America. But we knew without a doubt that the Lord wanted us to accept this assignment. This is where He wants us—for now."

I knelt on the aging carpet, bowed my head to the floor, and surrendered my life completely to the Master. God sanctified me wholly.

The year 2001 brought two more milestones in Marty's life. First, at the Kansas City District Assembly in August, General Superintendent Jerry Porter ordained him as an elder, climaxing a decade-long process of preparation and study that started with a call on the mission field. Second, he was promoted to the position of director of Candidate Development and Volunteerism, which includes both Work and Witness and Nazarenes in Volunteer Service, two areas about which he is passionate.

"I'm thankful for the privilege I have to help people fulfill their call through Work and Witness and NIVS as I did," says Marty. "And I'm grateful for a church that believes in missions and for people, such as Louie, Craig, and Herb who believed in me and were willing to give me a chance."

But there's one more important part of Marty's story to be told. "On my first Work and Witness trip when I was called to missions," Marty says, "I encountered God in another life-changing way. One night in a hotel room in the middle of Ecuador, our team met for a time of devotions. Louie spoke and gave his testimony. The Holy Spirit had been dealing with me about my total commitment to God. That night, along with three others, I knelt on the aging carpet, bowed my head to the floor, and surrendered my life completely to the Master. God sanctified me wholly, filling me with His Spirit. From that point on I didn't have to worry about what the future held. I knew He was in control—and He still is to this day."

Work and Witness impact? Just consider the miracles in Marty's story . . . a call to missions . . . the experience of entire sanctification . . . an NIVS assignment . . . Debbie, his future wife . . . specialized and career missionary appointments . . . a call to preach . . . their son's birth on the mission field . . . coordinating Work and Witness teams for a decade in South America . . . ordination as an elder . . . serving the Church of the Nazarene as director of missionary candidate development and volunteerism.

"You never know what may happen on a Work and Witness trip," Marty declares. "I challenge you: try one. It may be a life-changing experience for you too!"

A Difference-Making Maverick

Truck driver. Welder. Businessman. Builder. Contractor. Pastor. Evangelist. Don McBride's list of jobs reads like the yellow pages.

Don, a retired elder, met Larry and Judy Webb, soon-to-be-retired missionaries at a faith promise weekend in Nampa Karcher Church of the Nazarene in Idaho. And this chance—no, providential—meeting made a far-reaching impact that took Don all the way to Bolivia.

Don listened intently as Larry shared about his and Judy's work in this landlocked nation in South America. The missionary described the fascinating country—glacial ice and snow of the high Andes . . . hot, sticky Amazon jungles . . . the altiplano at 13,000 feet . . . the picturesque Cochabamba Valley with its perpetually spring climate . . . the Aymara Indians, a pre-Incan culture, still plowing with oxen to plant potatoes.

Among the pictures that Larry painted that evening was one of the Pasto Grande, a Bolivian project to help retired pastors and widows of ministers. Political and economic factors had devastated the ability of the Bolivian Nazarene Pastors' Retirement

Fund to respond to the financial needs of the growing number of retirees. In the distribution of benefits, some widows received as little as $3 (U.S.) per month, while the pastor with the greatest number of years of service would get slightly more than $20.

Pasto Grande is a unique place on the altiplano where irrigation has brought in abundant crops of onions and carrots—up to 500 bags per acre. At $8 per bag, this brings in $4,000 of gross income for each acre plot. With help from Nazarene Compassionate Ministries and a matching individual donation, the project acquired 12 acres and when fully operational will provide a place where widows or retired pastors can build a home, live rent free, and enjoy the harvest of their personal gardens. The project residents, who desire to do so, can share in the annual division of the irrigated cropland, keeping 75 percent of the harvest with 25 percent reverting to the project to maintain pumps, pay electric bills, and purchase additional acreage.

As Larry finished that part of the Friday evening presentation, he said: "Widows can plant onions, widows can irrigate onions, and widows can harvest onions. The big challenge is the plowing and preparation of the cropland."

All who know Don recognize he is the type that manifests a bit of a *maverick* streak.

Don heard those words and pondered them through the night. In the morning he laid a colored photograph of a bright red Massey-Ferguson tractor on the Webbs' display table. "Larry, this is what you need

27

for the project," Don said matter-of-factly. Little did the retiree realize how God would bring that photo into reality and allow him to be a primary subject in the picture.

At the Saturday morning men's breakfast, Larry focused on the impact that Work and Witness has had on world evangelism in the Church of the Nazarene. He extended an invitation to participate in the "Maverick" program to construct a multiphase district campground-retreat center at Cliza, Bolivia. "I chose the word *maverick*," Larry said, "to include the many talented individuals who are unable to participate with regular teams or perhaps from a church that could never sponsor a team."

Don had been on previous church-related projects in the United States, so he wasn't a novice. And all who know Don recognize he is the type that manifests a bit of a *maverick* streak. The missionary's presentation resonated with his own heart's desires. But as a retired minister, Don had to live with economic realities. Overseas trips cost money.

"I decided that morning I should commit to the project," Don says, "although I didn't know where the funds would come from." As he picked up a Maverick application and prepared to fill it out, he was impressed to call David Hills and invite him to go along. (David, a successful businessman, had been nurtured as a teen in one of Don's earlier pastorates.)

"Still, there was the matter of money," Don says. "Yet I knew that God has the resources; so, when I went home, I felt at peace about my decision.

"I had been in an accident in Washington that had never been settled," Don continues. "When I picked up our mail at 2:00 that afternoon, there was a check from the insurance company for nearly $1,200, which was definite confirmation of the decision made four hours earlier. Then gifts started coming in—from family, friends, church folks—that ranged from a candy bar to $500. Though I never asked for help, I was surprised when the total came to more than $1,000. I still marvel at this miracle.

After taking just one shower, the Mavericks vowed this was one area in which they could and would make an impact.

Six weeks after that providential faith promise event, the very first Maverick team flew to Cliza. Joining missionaries Larry and Judy Webb were Don and two others from Idaho, three men from New York, a single youth from New Mexico, a father and preteen son from Alaska.

Arriving at the work site, the team enjoyed a flavorful Bolivian lunch and took a much-appreciated siesta. (Team members had been traveling 24 hours or longer.) This is a custom the Mavericks agreed they could adapt to quite easily.

The ground floor of the three-story facility, though unfinished, could still be used as a dormitory. Surveying the status of the project, the group listed 25 jobs, including a solar heating system for the showers. The water coming from the ground is about 58 degrees, rather chilly for a bath. The team quickly discovered that only one of the two showers had warm water, an "exotic" electric type with wiring that tended to spook North Americans. When operating, the warmth of the water was inversely proportionate to the volume. At low volume the electric shower provided warm water, but not much shower. As the water volume is increased, the temperature drops accordingly. After taking just one shower, the Mavericks vowed this was one area in which they could and would make an impact.

By the time Maverick teams 1 and 2 left Cliza, 23 of the 25 tasks had been completed, including the solar water system.

From the Maverick's food budget, enough money was skimmed to buy a truckload of bricks, sand, and cement for the Pasto Grande project. The excited members—minus David who had to return home unexpectedly—squeezed their luggage and tools

Larry Webb working on the solar water system

30

Don McBride *(left)* and Richard Willard at Cliza

along with themselves into a chartered bus to travel to Pasto Grande. This 10-hour round-trip across the Andes Mountains in one day proved to be arduous, to say the least.

"Though the 13,000-foot altiplano may be home for the Aymara Indians," Larry says, "and a great place to play soccer, it's a real challenge for gringos from San Diego and other low altitude places." While the Bolivian locals labored hard mixing cement and laying bricks, the Mavericks did their best to keep busy as "helpers" while gasping and stopping often to get their breath.

During his time at Pasto Grande, Don caught a vision for the project. He saw the dire need for a deep well as a water source, a water tower, and of course, a tractor. He strolled through fields of carrots and onions, marveling at the production potential when irrigation became available. He snapped roll after roll of film, capturing the scenes that impressed and impacted him.

Back in Idaho, he shared his enthusiasm for what the Mavericks had accomplished at both Cliza and Pasto Grande.

Although David Hills had missed the trip to Pasto Grande, Don succeeded in communicating to his friend his excitement for the project. The following year David invited Larry Webb to request funds from a foundation with which he (David) is involved. The proposal was written, accepted, and granted, and as a result Pasto Grande received a $25,000 check for the purchase of a tractor.

"Yes, widows can plant onions," Larry reminds us, "and widows can irrigate onions and widows can harvest onions, but a tractor will prepare the ground.

"Thanks, Dave, for being sensitive to the gentle nudging of the Spirit," Larry says. "What you and others like you have done will make an impact for years to come.

"And thanks, Don. Thanks for your courage to go and share your vision with others. You are truly a difference-making Maverick."

A Long-Lasting Harvest

The persistent ringing of the telephone pierced the balmy night air. It was two o'clock in the morning of October 10, 1996. As a missionary in the Philippines, Dave Hane knew a telephone call at that hour meant one of two things: a wrong number or urgent news from home. He suspected the former; it was the latter. His dad was gone.

For Dave the next few days rushed by in a blur as he hurried to the family homestead in Oklahoma for the funeral and grieved with his mother, brothers, and other family members and friends. While his emptiness and loneliness were overwhelming, Dave was comforted in the assurance his father was rejoicing with the Lord.

"As we tried to adjust to the loss in the weeks that followed," Dave says, "an oft-repeated saying of Dad's kept running through my mind: 'Only one life will soon be past; only what's done for Christ will last.'[1] Both Dad and Mom always lived with eternity in view."

Dave knew that nothing would please his father more than to establish a memorial fund to build a

---

1. Taken from the poem "Only One Life." Author unknown.

church in his honor somewhere in the Asia-Pacific Region. But three years would pass before he found out where "somewhere" was.

✻　✻　✻

Five miles from the Myanmar border, Banmai Patana is one of the many Red Lahu tribal villages scattered across northwestern Thailand. The residents of this remote mountain settlement are primarily slash-and-burn farmers, growing their crops on the steep slopes and narrow fertile valleys of the border mountain range.

The Red Lahu are known as theistic animists who are waiting for the Creator of the universe to reveal himself to them. Because they cannot find the Creator, they worship various spirits. Each family has a corner in their homes devoted to their animistic worship where they burn incense and offer food in an attempt to appease the various spirits that haunt their daily lives. (Note: Once the Red Lahu find God the Creator, they cease their animistic worship practices.)

In 1999 Rev. Jasuh Jana[2] moved to Banmai Patana to plant the first Christian church. "When I first met Jasuh," Dave says, "I was impressed by two things: his quiet, humble spirit and his burning desire to take the gospel to the Lahu. As a former witch doctor, Jasuh had been his village's connection to the spirit world. When the people needed guidance, he

---

2. Jasuh's dramatic conversion story was told in the 2002-2003 reading NMI book *Hands for the Harvest* and the 2000 video *A Thai Tapestry*.

called on the spirits to show him what to do. But now as a Nazarene pastor, Jasuh felt a heavy responsibility to introduce his people to the true Creator God whom they had been seeking for centuries."

The beginning days of planting the church in Banmai Patana were difficult, and progress was slow. The first big break came when missionary Sam Yangmi's compassion and love impressed the village headman. Rev. Yangmi's impact and Jasuh's arrival, along with the showing of the *JESUS* film and other evangelistic crusades, resulted in many people—including the village headman—making public commitments to turn from their old ways to worship the true Creator. Soon 42 villagers, after destroying their spirit shelves and charms, received Christian baptism in a nearby irrigation canal.

The Body of Believers was quickly growing. Although the group had been meeting in a bamboo-and-thatched-roof arbor, which also served as the pastor's dining room, a more adequate house of worship was urgently needed.

"Banmai Patana seemed like the perfect place to have a church built in Dad's memory," Dave says. "It was a rural farming community where even the red soil called to mind the red shale dirt found in parts of Oklahoma."

Since Dave knew Jasuh, he wanted to do more than just send money for a building. He wanted to become involved himself—to be a part of the impact. A memorial Work and Witness seemed like the perfect solution. Dreams turned into plans.

"My wife, Kim, and our five-year-old son, Jonathan, joined me in this venture," Dave says. "We invited fellow missionaries from the Asia-Pacific regional office and the Asia-Pacific Nazarene Theological Seminary (APNTS) to be part of the team. And to help expand their worldview, three seminary students received funds to participate." With great excitement and anticipation, Dave began to work on the project's details with Sam Yangmi. Now, the plans, built upon dreams, turned into action.

The members felt their first day on the job must have been like the Tower of Babel project.

"Since we knew nothing of construction methods in Thailand," Dave admits, "we decided we should work closely with a six-member Thai con-

Dave Hane *(middle)* working with Mr. Wat *(right)* and David Ackerman from APNTS

Pastor Jasuh laying bricks for his church

struction crew, especially since they were experienced." These builders had helped with other church projects on the district. The foreman, Nanthawat Jantib, was a Buddhist, as are 94 percent of the people of Thailand.

"We shortened his name to Mr. Wat," Dave says. "He was a skilled and patient man, having worked with 'foreign' Work and Witness teams before."

Mr. Wat spoke no English, and the Work and Witness team spoke no Thai. The members felt their first day on the job must have been like the Tower of Babel project. "We were afraid the results would be the same as well," Dave confesses. "But we soon learned Thai words for mortar, bricks, hammer, and nails, and the church began to 'grow' brick by brick."

Most of the team members were inexperienced in laying bricks; therefore, their rising walls were subject to frequent examinations by Inspector Wat.

If his one-word judgment was "snake," it meant the wall was not straight and needed more vigorous tapping to get it back in line. A "no snake" label meant the bricklayers were free to continue and subject to less frequent scrutiny as the week progressed.

While some folks mixed mortar, laid bricks, and fitted premade windows into openings, others held daily Vacation Bible School sessions with the ever-present curiosity-seeking village children. The pastor's daughter, a Bible college student, served as an adept interpreter of Bible stories and object lessons. "As the children eagerly soaked up the stories," Dave says, "we were overwhelmed by the thought they would be the first generation of children in Banmai Patana to grow up in a Christian village with an active, vibrant church." A Work and Witness miracle!

Rev. Yangmi and Pastor Jasuh used the irrigation ditch to baptize six additional believers.

Yet, the ministry was to more than children. Mr. Wat's wife, Kesorn, had planned to stay only for the first day. However, after making friends with team members, she decided to stay the rest of the week, helping prepare meals and refreshments and participating in many of the children's activities. Through the Bible stories and lessons, Kesorn heard the clear presentation of the gospel. "We prayed earnestly that the seed planted in her heart would grow and lead her into a personal relationship with Christ," Dave reports.

Midway through the week, the district *JESUS*

film team arrived. Although many in Banmai Patana had seen the film previously, it still held great interest not only to unbelievers but also to new Christians who were still unfamiliar with the stories of Jesus' life. At the close of the film, several more responded to accept Christ. The next morning, Rev. Yangmi and Pastor Jasuh used the irrigation ditch to baptize six additional believers. After the ritual, the new Christians invited the team to participate in removing and burning various objects in their houses associated with spirit worship. What a blessing it was for team members to see children's Bible story pictures displayed in prominent places on the bamboo walls of the villagers' houses. More impact. More miracles.

"How fitting that our last Sunday in Banmai Patana was Easter Sunday," Dave says. "The Resurrection theme was evident everywhere—in the gentle smile of Jasuh, the former witch doctor; in the faces

James H. Hane memorial church in Thailand

of new Lahu believers who just the week before were living in the dark fear of the spirit world; in the empty cross that decorated the front of the church building; in the joyous thought of seeing Dad again someday."

Before departing the village, Dave asked Jasuh, "If you had the chance this morning to speak to every Lahu village, what would you tell them?"

The pastor's answer was simple. "This life is temporal. There is such a thing as eternity. If you want eternal life, it's available only through Christ."

Jasuh's words were especially significant in light of the plaque on the back wall of his newly completed church:

**This church is built in celebration of
James H. Hane,
an Oklahoma farmer who planted
seeds of eternal significance,
honored here by his wife and three sons.
April 23, 2000
"Only one life will soon be past;
Only what's done for Christ will last."**

Dave Hane boarded the plane for the flight back to Manila with his fellow team members. "As I reflected on this memorable trip to Thailand," Dave says, "I was filled with a deep sense of accomplishment. Dad had planted the wheat crop on our family farm in the fall of 1996, but he wasn't with us for the harvest the following spring. But now a church stands in his memory in a hill-tribe village in northwestern Thailand that will be bringing in the harvest for many years to come. And that is the one that will last—a long-lasting harvest."

A Missionary-Calling Journey

"Why can't I take these boxes too?" Roxanne said, her fingers tapping a steady beat on the airport counter. "We've got to have them! We really do!" Her voice dripped with agitation. "I'll pay the extra money. Just let me take them. *Now!*"

Roxanne's desperate pleas did not move the apparent hardened resolve of the airline personnel. Precious seconds ticked away as attempts at negotiation failed. Roxanne, along with Cort and Karen Miller, watched as the 747 backed away from the gate, leaving the three staring helplessly, angrily, and wondering when—or if—they would ever meet up with their other team members in Miami.

Roxanne Alexander was leading a medical Work and Witness team to the Dominican Republic (D.R.). Sponsored by Nazarene Health Care Fellowship (NHCF), this was Roxanne's fourth trip to the D.R., and she was very familiar with the assignment. Yet she tingled with excitement as she prayed and planned for this new experience. She looked forward to seeing longtime friends and making new ones.

The 16-member team from various cities in the United States consisted of a medical doctor and his wife, 4 registered nurses (RNs), 2 student RNs, and 8 non-health-care individuals. A few were first-timers. The group would connect with nationals, including a medical doctor, in Santo Domingo, D.R.'s capital.

In preparing for this latest adventure, Roxanne had phoned and E-mailed the volunteers countless times. She felt as if they were old friends, even though they had not yet met face-to-face. She could hardly wait.

And now this latest setback. "O God," Roxanne prayed silently, yet with a sense of urgency. "Please, please help us. This trip is Your doing. Help us get to Miami."

I vowed not to look in a mirror again until I got home.

Back at the Kansas City airline counter, more pleas, more negotiation, more prayers. Suddenly, the trio found themselves aboard the next flight to southern Florida—without the boxes. As the plane soared at 30,000 feet, Roxanne sat nervously, unable to relax, worrying about the timing of their arrival in Miami. "God, I know You are sovereign," she prayed again. "I trust You to work out the details of this trip according to Your will. I leave it in Your hands."

As the jet touched down and gated in Miami, the three deplaned and raced to link up with the others. Then Roxanne learned that storms along the east coast caused most flights to be delayed, detaining other team members as well. When she found her team, they were sitting calmly and waiting patiently for their leader to join them. Another miracle.

The team, now intact, set out on the last leg of the journey to the mission field. Two hours later, they landed in the D.R. The air hung thick with humidity; the heat still oppressed even though the sun had set long before. "I knew that any attention to my hair and makeup would be wasted effort," Roxanne says. "I vowed not to look in a mirror again until I got home."

The team then encountered the "customs challenge," especially getting the medical supplies through the red tape. The process was going smoothly, when suddenly a uniformed agent motioned for Roxanne to put her bags on the table for examination. "My heart sank," she says. "My mind raced through possible consequences of his demand. Confiscation? Fine? What else?"

She and Cort heaved one of the weighty bags up for inspection—a huge tote filled with medicines and medical supplies. When Roxanne unzipped the bag, the agent looked at her, rolled his eyes, and spat out an unrepeatable comment. When she told him about the contents and their purpose, he responded, "I . . . don't . . . know." He paused, seemingly contemplating his options, the time passing with agonizing slowness. Then he said with a flip of his hand, "Oh, go on."

The team affectionately dubbed their team leader "Mama Roxanna," and she cherished her charges as a mother lion does her young cubs.

Relieved and elated, Roxanne thanked the agent and uttered a sincere, "God bless you." The response was a surprising, "Yes, He does."

Indeed He does, Roxanne thought, lifting a hushed praise. She motioned to the rest of the team behind her that she had successfully cleared this hurdle. One by one each passed through customs with baggage and supplies intact. One more miracle!

Dr. Carlos and Rosa Saenz, Paquito Bido, and several others met the team outside the airport. (Carlos is the Nazarene Compassionate Ministries [NCM] coordinator for the Caribbean Region and director for the Spanish-speaking Caribbean Field. Paquito Bido is the NCM coordinator for the D.R.) "What a warm welcome we received—both from the

Mama Roxanna with some of the kids in Dominican Republic

people and the weather!" Roxanne says. "And how grateful we were to see our dear friends once again!"

The team affectionately dubbed their team leader "Mama Roxanna," and she cherished her charges as a mother lion does her young cubs. By the time the group arrived at their quarters, which was a Work and Witness house, it was about 10:00 P.M. "What a relief! We had arrived," Roxanne says. "But relaxation was momentary. We had to work late into the evening, preparing supplies and clarifying assignments for the next day. Much later when I finally got to bed, even the weight of the humidity could not steal away my much-appreciated slumber."

The next morning the team arose before sunrise, ate a quick breakfast, and boarded an older model, open-windowed bus for the trip to the project site for that day. They traveled for about two hours, the women's hair flying in the wind. "This inconvenience resulted in a 'bad hair day,'" Roxanne admits, "but it was either tangled hair or suffocating heat. And we chose matted tresses."

The clinic was set up in a church, as it was most days. The entry served as the registration area, the platform functioned as the pharmacy, and the pews became cubicles for treatment.

"The team melded the first day as if we had been working together for years," Roxanne says. "Everyone cooperated so well. There was not a grouch or whiner in the bunch. The non-health-care individuals worked alongside the physicians and nurses—registering patients, assisting with treatment, hauling supplies, dispensing medications, doing whatever-needed-to-be-done tasks. Some provided a half-day Bible school activity for children in the church and surrounding community.

"We worked hard, laughed hard, cried hard," says Roxanne. "There certainly was no time for boredom." Todd, one of the single nurses, received a marriage proposal from a woman with six children. "We still laugh about that one," Roxanne comments. "But Mama Roxanna was there and helped Todd wiggle out of that dilemma."

"I have to do something," Cort says, "for the need is so huge."

In six days the team treated more than 700 people. Their service complete, these medical volunteers returned to their homes and normal routines—but not the same. Each one gained a lifetime of memories in just a week; each one was a whole lot richer.

* * *

How did this particular trip impact the participants? A few share their thoughts.

Cort and Karen Miller feel their experience in D.R. confirmed God's call to cross-cultural work, somewhere, sometime. "I first sensed God's leading on a CAUSE (Colleges and Universities Serving and Enabling) trip to Peru while a student at MidAmerica Nazarene University (MNU)," Cort says. "That trip put a strong desire in my heart for serving others that has never abated." After graduation, he enrolled in Nazarene Theological Seminary and last year was awarded a master's in missiology. He's now

Karen and Cort Miller

working on an M.B.A. degree in international business. As an employee for Nazarene Compassionate Ministries, he is the coordinator for communication and development.

Karen, also an MNU graduate, has earned a master's at Southern Nazarene University and a Ph.D. from the University of Missouri at Kansas City. She is now chair of the English and Psychology Division at Avila University in Kansas City. She shares her husband's passion to serve the Lord in cross-cultural ministry. Both of the Millers have been deeply involved in an ESL (English as a second language) program at their church as implementers, teachers, and directors.

"I have to do something," Cort says, "for the need is so huge. As we visited different villages in the D.R., observing the abject poverty there and seeing people who are helpless to do anything about their plight, Karen and I were greatly impacted. We saw teens and adults with deformities and handicaps that could have been corrected earlier in their lives if health care had been available. Both of us remain open to God as He directs our lives and our future, certainly in cross-cultural ministry."

✳ ✳ ✳

"On this trip to the Dominican Republic," nurse Abigail Stein says, "I became keenly aware of how valuable the doctor's role is in this environment. I learned that the people don't receive consistent health care and many we treated were receiving their very first doctor's visit." Abigail observed first-hand how much more a doctor is able to do than a nurse and that an RN is limited in health care outside a hospital or clinic.

"My heart felt a burden to travel to remote villages and provide complete health care, teach the gospel, and offer hope to the people," Abigail says. "I left D.R. with a renewed affirmation to fulfill God's calling as a missionary. *But how?*" I wondered.

Abigail soon had the answer to her question. A nearby college sent her information about a graduate degree program that included a family nurse practitioner (FNP) degree. "An FNP is capable of diagnosing diseases, prescribing medications, and treating the complete needs of patients," Abigail says, "which is perfect for the care I'd like to provide." She enrolled and will soon complete the program. "Now, I'm just waiting and praying for God to guide my future. I would love to be an FNP missionary in the Dominican Republic—or anywhere God wants me—and whenever it fits into His plan and timing for my life."

❊ ❊ ❊

"I returned to my home in Olathe, Kansas," Roxanne says, "but my trip to the D.R. was not over. Four days later I became ill with dengue fever—a mosquito bite the culprit—that resulted in a week-long hospital stay. Because of the nature of dengue, the doctors were not familiar with the symptoms, and I left the hospital without an official diagnosis." Though she had a rough time physically, when asked if she'd go again, she said, "In a heartbeat!"

And since this trip, the Lord has continued to work in Roxanne's life. "God's call upon my life in unexpected ways led me to apply to the World Mission Department for missionary service," she says. In 2002 Roxanne was appointed to a two-year missionary intern contract. Today, she is in Ukraine, giving support to the mission personnel there, and serving as the Nazarene Compassionate Ministries coordinator for the CIS (Commonwealth of Independent States) Field.

"I only desire to be used of God wherever He leads," she says, "even to the uttermost parts of the earth—and that includes Ukraine."

Does Work and Witness have an impact? You be the judge.

A Walking-to-Africa Venture

"Venezuela? Really, Dad?" Alex said, hoping this wasn't a joke.

"Yes, Son. I'd like our entire family to take a missions trip to South America."

"When? How soon can we leave?" the 12-year-old insisted. His boyish enthusiasm like a geyser spewed forth in both voice and demeanor. "When, Dad? Now? I want to go *right now!*"

"Hold on there, Alex. Not right away . . . probably in a couple of years when I can take a sabbatical. We'll need to save our money."

Alex Mahaffey was so excited he could hardly sleep or eat or do anything—even though it was two years away. All he could think about was the big journey. Right away he began to think about ways to earn money.

Soon he and his older brother, Robert, found a job with a realtor to distribute flyers in their city. "We walked and walked and walked," Alex says. Countless miles. Endless hours. Off and on, month after month after month. "It was hard work, for sure," he admits. "But the prospects of the trip kept us trudging in the Texas heat. And we were able to save most of the money we earned."

Two years later, anticipation turned to frustration. Grace Church of the Nazarene in Nashville extended a call to Alex's father to become their pastor. Feeling this was God's will, the Mahaffeys moved to Tennessee. The dream trip to Venezuela was aborted.

"Sure, I was disappointed," Alex admits. "But I knew this is what the Lord wanted. Little did I realize the significance of this move and how it would affect my future."

Three years later, the Tennessee District planned a Work and Witness trip to Africa. "I still had the money I'd stashed away, thanks to all that walking," Alex says, "so I signed up. I had always dreamed of going to Africa, and now it would be a reality."

Alex at Africa Nazarene University

Alex was the only teen volunteer on the W&W team from the Volunteer State. Their task? To help construct a building at Africa Nazarene University in Kenya. "What a great group of workers," Alex says. "The best part, they were all Christians."

This trip impacted Alex, then 17 years old, in numerous ways. "I saw everything," he says, "from God's wondrous creation to the sadness of extreme poverty. We went on a safari where I saw animals in their natural habitat that I had only dreamed of. We were within yards of lions, giraffes, hippos, zebras, gazelles, and other creatures usually caged in zoos. I almost had to pinch myself to make sure I wasn't fantasizing.

The mighty power of God astounded Alex as he observed the Creator's handiwork—from microscopic ants to mammoth hippos, from stunning sunsets to majestic mountains.

"On the flip side, we visited Nairobi and saw people begging for anything we might give them —and even some things we wouldn't part with. I didn't realize how blessed I was until seeing the street people in Nairobi. The memory still haunts and impacts me."

The mighty power of God astounded Alex as he observed the Creator's handiwork—from microscopic ants to mammoth hippos, from stunning sunsets to majestic mountains. "I realized on this trip how much God protects me," Alex says. "One of the most thrilling adventures, rafting on the Nile River, happened on a later trip. The immense power of the river's current was incredible, even frightening, and yet no one received a scratch. God was watching over us."

Alex feels that his interaction with people was the most valuable part of the W&W experience to Kenya. For example, he met Fortune, a young man about his age. "As we talked we found out we had a lot in common," Alex says. "We were both planning to major in religion and held many of the same views. One evening we met together for a long time, shared our testimonies, prayed together, and encouraged each other in our walk with Christ. I will never forget that night. I'm really looking forward to seeing Fortune again, and I know I will. Maybe not here, and maybe not there in Africa. But one day we *will* meet again!

"God used this trip to shape and form me, to work some miracles in my life," Alex testifies. "An important lesson for me was that God is working not just here in the United States or in my life, but He is working everywhere, that His salvation and hope are universal. It was good to see for myself that the African people, whose culture and lifestyle are so different than mine, worship the same God I do. All of a sudden, I understood that my way of living is not the only way of living, that material things are not what really matters."

Since participating in this long-delayed excursion, Alex has been on three more overseas mission trips: to Peru with his church youth group, to Papua New Guinea with his church, and to Uganda with a CAUSE (Colleges and Universities Serving and Enabling) team from Trevecca Nazarene University.

Alex with new friends in Kenya

And he is hoping to go again, somewhere, in the summer of 2003 after graduation.

"I love missions," he says, "and would jump at the chance to serve on the mission field if God would choose to call me. I'm willing to go wherever He leads me, and I'm excited for His plan to be executed in my life.

"As you can see, Work and Witness is awesome!" Alex says. "It definitely gave me a heart for missions. I still remember vividly those scorching Texas days when I thought I was only walking door-to-door to deliver real-estate advertisements. Actually, I was walking to Africa—and beyond!"

An Unforgettable Serendipity

I wonder what he's doing now? Gary wondered when he finished reading the "Little Lost Lamb" from the mission book *Favorites of Helen Temple.*

According to the story, a six-year-old Indian boy in Guatemala was sold by his father to satisfy his craving for alcohol. Through a miracle of God's grace, the lad's uncle found him and willingly paid three times the selling price to buy him back. Overjoyed to be back with his mother and siblings, the boy learned his father had died. One day in a church service, the youth heard the parable of the prodigal son, which was illustrated with colorful flannelgraph figures. The boy was touched when he realized the true love of a father for a son, and he quickly opened his heart to the Heavenly Father.

Years later as a young adult, Feliciano Sep felt God's call to Christian service. He enrolled in Instituto Biblico Nazareno (Nazarene Bible Institute) in Cobán. An outstanding soloist, Feliciano developed his love for music and learned to play several instruments—guitar, accordion, piano, and organ—and to direct a choir.

Betty Sadat, Nazarene missionary, was impressed with Feliciano's preaching and language abilities. She asked him to be part of a team to help finish the translation of the Bible that her husband, William, had started before God called him home. Feliciano gladly joined the team to help his own people, the Pokomchís, to receive God's Word.

✳ ✳ ✳

Little did Gary dream that he would ever meet the young boy who was sold by his father and later became a Nazarene leader in Guatemala. Although the story fascinated and impacted Gary, the main character was just another person in a foreign country someplace. Or was he?

The man from the pages of an NMI reading book had suddenly come to life.

Gary Hasenauer joined a 22-member Work and Witness team from the New Mexico District that planned a trip to Guatemala with a twofold purpose: to refurbish a church and to transform a bus into a medical clinic. Stan Yocom, a team member, drove a used school bus more than 2,000 miles down through Mexico and into Guatemala, while the others flew into Guatemala City.

Arriving in Cobán, a small city in the mountains of central Guatemala, Gary had a surprise. In fact, an unforgettable surprise—indeed, a miracle. He learned that he would be working with Feliciano Sep, the national leader of the team. The man from the pages of an NMI reading book had suddenly come to life.

The first morning, Feliciano led the New Mexico

Feliciano Sep with his wife and son

folks through the narrow city streets and on to the one-lane road carved out of the cloud-covered mountainside. They made their way to Chilley Church of the Nazarene, where Rev. Sep had pastored for 10 years.

People were everywhere. Many had been waiting since early morning for this first-ever clinic. The women and girls were attired in bright, colorful blouses and full skirts, and most wore rubber shoes. The men and boys wore typical shirts and trousers and sported rubber boots. While the team wondered about the unusual footwear, they learned that this area of the country has an average of 200 inches of rain each year. Leather shoes would be impractical; they would never, never last.

As the team surveyed the situation in the village, they determined the bus would be best for dental work. The church, which seated about 300, would serve as the medical clinic. John Carson and his assistant, Colin Elito, worked in the bus with dental patients. Their hours were jam-packed with little time for rest. In one day alone they pulled 96 teeth. Pastor Cecil Kimberlin from New Mexico and Frankie Elliot ran the bus lab and helped with blood pressure checks whenever they could.

For the medical clinic Gloria and Ramón Gallegos, team members from the Santa Fe, New Mexico, church received the assignment to line up the people who had been given numbers—to the best of their ability, of course. The fact that the Gallegoses spoke Spanish was of immense value. Dr. Helmer Juarez, a Nazarene medical doctor from Guatemala, and two missionary nurses set up medical stations inside the church on the wooden benches.

When Gary used a felt-tip pen and drew a pair of feet on the scales, success was immediate.

Gary and Mary K. Frazier were responsible for weighing people and administering two pills. Trying to get the patients to chew the medicine proved to be a challenge. These "nurses" had to rely on sign language until a Spanish-Pokomchí speaker gave them the words they needed. *"Tecush comen* worked wonders!" Gary says.

Showing people how to stand on scales for a weight check also provided a problem. When Gary used a felt-tip pen and drew a pair of feet on the scales, success was immediate. "Nobody was over-

Gary Hasenauer weighing a Pokomchí girl

weight," Gary says. "The people's diet and their mountain walking obviously made the difference."

While the medical part of the "work" was happening, Ron Field, the New Mexico Work and Witness coordinator, led the construction part of the "work." Ron and several helpers built pews and laid floor tiles for the El Esfuerzo Church.

Communication provided an ongoing dilemma, as interpretation was needed in three languages: English, Spanish, and Pokomchí. The team survived with local people and the team members who knew Spanish. The church youth stopped by the work site every afternoon on the way from school. "My Spanish was limited," Gary admits, "but a good Spanish-English dictionary with Guatemalan idioms was a big hit. We laughed a lot as we tried to 'read' each other's language. But through our frustrations and laughter, we felt the bond of God's love."

The New Mexicans discovered that the battery in Feliciano's car frequently "died" and the 400 quetzales (U.S.$50) needed to replace the battery was beyond his family's means. "When we learned Rev. Sep's need," Gary says, "our team quickly donated the amount and then located a battery that would fit his vehicle. What a thrill to see the thankfulness on Feliciano's countenance and sense the heartfelt appreciation of his family."

Later, the team learned that Feliciano was put in charge of finishing the Old Testament translation in Pokomchí. He received special courses from the Wycliff School of Linguistics and American Bible Society.

"How blessed I was to be able to see for myself the continuing chapters of a story I had read in one of our missionary books years ago," Gary says. "A surprise? Certainly. But our Lord often surprises those who trust and obey Him. Meeting Feliciano Sep was an impacting serendipity—one I shall always remember and cherish."

A Finding-God Experience

"Look for God in the activities of today," Jeff Croft challenged, as he closed the Monday morning devotional. "Then be ready to share this evening in our debriefing time." The group dispersed to begin their assigned tasks for the day.

Jeff, associate pastor of First Church of the Nazarene in Anderson, Indiana, was the devotional leader of a 21-member team that had traveled to Nazarene Indian Bible College (NIBC) in Albuquerque, New Mexico. Each morning as the group met before the day's work, Jeff gave a homily, basing his comments on selected concepts from the book *The God Chasers* by Tommy Tenney. The author explores how God-fearing people through the ages—from Moses and Paul to A. W. Tozer and Leonard Ravenhill—have found God. Then Jeff posed the all-important question to the team: "Where can you find God today?" He added, "Look for His miracles in the mundane events of your life."

The varied work tasks, sometimes routine but at times quite challenging, included changing a window into a door through a two-foot thick wall . . . running new power lines . . . converting a garage into a print-

The team members in a newly remodeled room

ing and cutting room . . . running, folding, addressing, stuffing, and sorting the NIBC newsletter . . . moving phone and computer lines . . . replacing an irrigation pump and storage tank . . . sorting and readying clothing for distribution . . . installing a new hot-water line that required some remodeling . . . helping in the day care . . . shredding obsolete documents . . . restocking the food pantry . . . preparing drywall for painting. An ongoing joke among those involved in the drywall project was, "Did I ever mention that I don't like doing mud work?"

> "It was like a scud missile had struck," one worker said, "and we weren't even at war."

One we-can't-believe-this-really-happened incident came while working on the irrigation pump and storage tank. In the replacement process, the tank slipped, bumped against the concrete-block pump house, and caved in the walls. "It was like a scud missile had struck," one worker said, "and we weren't even at war." Team members, led by Brank DeBruhl, spent the next few days rebuilding the walls, constructing a removable roof, and installing the new pump and tank, finishing only hours before Brank and a fellow worker left to return home.

At the end of each workday the team members gathered for a debriefing session. This unstructured time allowed the participants to share what they had experienced in the past several hours that had impacted them. These moments helped the group develop a sense of unity.

The first night Don indicated that God had spoken to him as he picked up a puppy, realizing that as he cradled the little dog in his arms he was also being embraced in the loving and strong arms of God. "The Lord reminded me," Don said, "that I am indeed helpless, but He was caring for my every need."

Another person had noted a flock of snow geese flying in their majestic V-shape formation in the winter sky overhead. These beautiful birds, rare to the visiting Hoosiers, symbolized God's blessings, His overwhelming goodness, day by day.

Linda fell in love with a student's craft, exquisite silver and turquoise jewelry, that helped pay for his education. She commissioned him to make a bracelet and arranged with school officials that the money would be applied to his school bill. Linda found God in the beautiful handiwork created by one of His own creations, a Native American silversmith.

Pastor Gary Cable and Jeff Croft *(standing l. to r.)*
with Irvin Shioshee, a Native American layman

One evening a man shared that he "just felt content." Everyone agreed. Then someone remarked that, for him, contentment presented a problem. "I don't want to be just content," he confessed. "I want to see the face of God." In the minutes that followed, God came with His special presence and touched the team members. Tears flowed and hearts melted as people opened their lives to the Lord. The Holy Spirit did His work—thoroughly, lovingly.

Later in the week when Beth, the team nurse, checked the blood pressure of a person in the group, she found it quite high. Gary Cable, senior pastor, and Beth rushed the worker to a hospital. She remained with the man throughout the day until medical attention was able to stabilize the abnormal pressure. *What a waste of my time,* Beth thought as she sat in the waiting room. *I'm letting the team down. I really should be helping the other ladies.*

Just the mention of snow geese caused Beth to beam.

Later, Jeff found Beth resting on a bench at the Bible school and noted she was not "looking" well. Her husband, John, verified his wife's emotional struggle, a feeling of insignificance and uselessness. Jeff sat down beside her. "You've done exactly what God needed you to do today," he commented. "And I believe God is preparing a special blessing for you. Just as you've been a blessing to others, God is going to bless you too."

Out of the corner of his eye, Jeff spotted a flight of snow geese. "Look there, Beth," he said, pointing upward, "and see the blessing, the miracle, God is already sending your way. And He is going to keep sending them." As the two watched in silence, hundreds upon hundreds of snow geese flew southward, blanketing the campus sky, creating an indelible, heartwarming picture. After returning to Indiana, just the mention of snow geese caused Beth to beam. She had found God in a couple of ways: through an act of kindness at an Albuquerque infirmary and in His marvelous migratory creation called snow geese.

One team member, a builder by profession, was a long-time Nazarene. However, Brad* had strayed from the Lord when he became involved in a relationship that started innocently but over time became an unhealthy one, causing pain and grief for several individuals. He knew this unwholesome relationship was keeping him at a distance from God and defeating him spiritually. By the end of the week in Albuquerque, Brad stood and testified, "Please pray for me. I'm under conviction, and I know I need to get my life straightened out. I'm . . . I'm just not ready . . . today."

As the team returned home, the Holy Spirit continued to impact Brad and deal with those issues that separated him from Christ. The very next Sunday, he went forward at the end of the service and knelt at the altar. Repenting of his sins and crying out for mercy, the Lord graciously forgave him. Brad found God and experienced His peace—a freedom-from-all-guilt peace—for the first time in months. As he surrendered everything to God, he was able to meet the Master face-to-face. And this miracle—this finding-God experience—started on a Work and Witness trip to serve Native Americans in the Southwest.

---

*Name has been changed.

An Impacting Project

"Hello, Dad. Would you like to go with us on a Work and Witness trip?"

"Where are you planning to go, Son?" Marvin responded.

"Not sure yet, but we've narrowed it down to three places. Possibly Panama."

"What will it cost?" Dad McKain queried.

"It's not settled, but we're trying to keep it under $1,000 a person. We're also raising $10,000 for building materials."

"When are you going?" Marvin continued the questioning.

"Looking at the last part of May next year."

That telephone call and brief conversation began a chain of events that would forever impact and change Marvin's life.

Mr. McKain's son Larry was then pastor of the Northland Community (now Tiffany Springs) Church of the Nazarene in north Kansas City. The young congregation was a new start, organized in the mid-1990s, with Dr. Larry McKain as its shepherd. During the first year, this mission-minded minister challenged his congregation, which was meeting in a school, to build a church on a mission field before they built their own facility. What a concept! What a generous, unselfish undertaking!

During the next three years, the congregation began a search for property of its own. Yet, even though some leads seemed promising, for one reason or another, all became proverbial dead ends, a rather discouraging circumstance for this fledgling group.

"Larry, remember what you said when we first started?" asked Christie Andersen, one of the charter members. "Don't you remember your challenge to us about building a church in another world area?"

The experience provided a taste for missions that Marvin rather liked.

Christie's questions jogged the pastor's memory and goaded his conscience. With the challenge renewed, the overseas mission trip rose to the top of ministry priorities. Once the decision was made, within a few weeks God provided the miracle of an ideal piece of property, and Northland Community congregation purchased it. (Really not a surprise, is it?)

Linda Phelps, the energetic NMI president, and Christie Andersen, the go-getter Work and Witness coordinator, took the project and ran—literally raced —with the idea. In a short time, plans were in place. Panama would be the destination. 'Twas then Pastor McKain phoned his father.

Marvin and his wife, Jo, had retired in 1991, and later moved to southern Missouri to be nearer their grandchildren. He had participated on another Work and Witness trip with the Greenville, South Carolina, First Church. The experience provided a taste for missions that Marvin rather liked. He decided to take another big bite by accompanying his son to Central America.

Over the next six months, Marvin's involvement in trip preparation was largely by remote control. The church sent him updates and instructions as the people raised money and finalized plans. Marvin sent in his money, renewed his passport, and drove to Kansas City a few times to attend Work and Witness rallies, planning sessions, and of course, to visit the grandkids.

Marvin McKain *(left)* **with missionary Peter Schroeder**

Marvin's final pretrip drive to Kansas City came on May 20, 1998. He joined Larry and the Northland Community group who left early the next day for the long flight to San José, Costa Rica. There, the 15-member team met up with Peter Schroeder, Nazarene missionary who would be their host, guide, and interpreter. They spent a day sightseeing and fellowshipping with missionaries.

After spending a night at the Nazarene seminary, the group boarded a bus for a six-hour journey over primitive roads, often crossing rivers by railroad bridges. Arriving in the town of Changuinola, Panama, they checked in to a motel, their headquarters for the next week. "A Hilton it wasn't," Marvin admits. "Not even Motel 6."

The next day, the team piled on a bus to transport them to the project site. The blacktop highway soon became a single-lane gravel road that snaked its way into the mountains. At the very end of the road was the village of Ojo de Agua. From here footpaths fanned out in various directions into the surrounding hills and peaks. The town consisted of a cluster of houses, a medical clinic, a parsonage/general store, and the Church of the Nazarene. There was no electricity except for one bulb and one outlet at the church, provided by a 600-watt motor generator. A single gravity-powered pipe brought water from a spring in the higher elevation.

The church facilities were a converted 14' x 40' chicken shed used for worship, a 12' x 12' fellowship hall that included an open cookhouse and fireplace, and an outhouse. The property also had a partially completed, 30' x 50' building that would be the focus of the team's efforts.

As the Americans and Panamanians worked side by side, it soon became apparent that the locals did not need the "foreigners" to construct the building. "They didn't need us," Marvin confesses. "Our group needed them to help us catch a new vision of world mission and how God was moving in third world countries. They helped us cement a new unity around what God wanted to do through Northland Community Church and showed us how people with so little could be so full of joy. They also helped us see how our priorities needed adjustment. I really needed that firsthand experience."

One evening at a rally of several churches in Changuinola, Larry preached—through an interpreter, of course. In his sermon he mentioned that Northland Community was still worshiping in a school, yet they felt God wanted them to build a church for someone else first. Larry asked the Panamanian Nazarenes to pray that the Lord would help the Kansas City congregation obtain the needed finances.

At the conclusion, the host pastor spoke with animation in Spanish—without an interpreter. The visitors from the States finally figured out what was happening when ushers went forward with offering plates and passed them only to their own people. The minister then addressed the guests, saying they would be praying for them and wanted to have a part in building their church back in Kansas City. He presented to Pastor Larry an offering of about $100 (U.S.).

Surprised. Overwhelmed. Humbled. Impacted. A mixture of emotions flooded the Northland Community team. When the group left Ojo de Agua, they left behind tools, clothes, money, and whatever they could for their new brothers and sisters in Christ.

To see a group of people with so little, worshiping in a chicken shed with such joy, moved me in a fresh, impacting way.

Steve Andersen, one of the team members, led the group in daily devotions. One evening he asked, "Is your heart broken for the lost? How would your priorities change if this were really true?"

That night the Lord spoke to Marvin specifically about the accumulation of things. "God clearly told me that I didn't need to accumulate any more, and that third-world-area churches were a good investment. In my corporate life, I had lived with key business concepts, such as 'return on investment,' 'return on assets,' 'rate of growth,' and others. I had always been part of churches with budgets of hundreds of thousands of dollars, but where few people were being added to the church. Then, in Panama, to see a group of people with so little, worshiping in a chicken shed with such joy, and winning their community and country-side for Christ moved me in a fresh, impacting way. And to understand that a $10,000 building would be the center of their community reinforced for me that 'little is much when God is in it.'"

This Work and Witness trip brought another significant change to Marvin and Jo as well. They fell so

The new church at Ojo de Agua

in love with the folks from Northland Community and the vision the church had for reaching the lost, they decided to become a part of this congregation. They moved to Kansas City in 1999 and joined this Great Commission church.

"We're having the time of our lives," Marvin reports. "And I look forward to being a part of another Work and Witness trip in the future."

Truly, an impacting project.

A Witnessing Discovery

Paris . . . city of lights and romance . . . high fashion and gourmet food . . . the Eiffel Tower and the Seine . . . the Louvre and the Mona Lisa . . . Notre Dame Cathedral and Arc d'Triomphe.

When Karen Robbins told her family and friends she was going to Paris on a Work and Witness trip, they were envious. When she tried to tell them this was a "working" trip, they responded with "sure," but the waving vocal intonation and winking eyes sent a message of incredulity.

By her own admission, Karen didn't fully know what the trip would be about. "I understood some of the 'work' we'd be doing—taping wallboard and painting," she says, "but I wondered how I would be a witness."

❋   ❋   ❋

The 20-member team from Ohio walked through an inner-city area of Paris, past small shops and little eateries, to a gated building with a sign that read "Eglise du Nazareen." Trevor Johnston, missionary in France, told the group on the bus ride from the airport they would be safe. "Guns are not allowed in France," he said, speaking in his natural

British accent, "hence there's little violent crime. But there will be the curious stares because you're a large group of people traveling together, and you obviously aren't from here. But you shouldn't have any problems like you might experience in the inner cities of the United States."

The team members walked through the gate, entered the building, and took stock of the work to be done in the old cinema being used by three different Nazarene congregations: a French-Caribbean group, an Arab-speaking church, and a Haitian assembly. Two Work and Witness teams had previously constructed walls to make rooms. This latest group would be the "finishers," but as the volunteers surveyed the inside, they observed that lots of finishing was still needed.

Due to a convention in Paris, Trevor had been unable to book hotel rooms close to the church. Therefore, the group had to travel by the Metro, Paris's subway, across the city each morning and evening. "After a few trips we noticed only rare smiles," Karen says. "One morning following devotions, we asked Trevor why the sullen faces."

"Let me tell you about their day," he responded. "Most of them get up very early and have more than an hour's ride on the crowded Metro to work. They work a full day, travel another hour to return home, eat a late supper, go to bed, and then start all over the next day. Anywhere you go in Paris there is traffic. You don't get anywhere quickly. And driving a car is even worse. Add to all this weariness the burdens they carry without Christ, you can understand why smiles are rare."

"I witnessed Trevor's tender heart for the Parisians over and over again," Karen said. "One evening as we strolled down the Champs Elysées, most of us were overwhelmed by the glitz and glamour. Trevor pointed out a famous restaurant, a popular place for movie stars, and whispered to the group, 'Look at the mother and child sitting just ahead of us. They are begging right here in the midst of all the chic patrons of the restaurants and fancy shops around us. This shows you something about the diverse people we serve.'"

Now ya gotta make it smooooth," Cecil said, using his best West Virginia drawl.

Throughout the week, team members labored hard, learning new skills and using old ones. When two team members had dropped out at the last minute, the Lord provided two talented men from another church, Cecil and Myrle, just 24 hours before leaving for Paris. Cecil was an expert at taping and spackling wallboard, the biggest job. "Now ya gotta make it smooooth," he said, using his best West Virginia drawl. "The smoooother ya make it, the less sandin' we hafta do."

As the week progressed, team members began to find their niche. Cecil taped and spackled, his specialty. Twila and Arla became quite good at taping, while Ponce became a perfectionist at sanding. Eunice climbed up on the scaffolding high above the sanctuary to paint the walls. Elaine and Karen tackled the painting at the "lower elevations." Walter and Myrle constructed a wall in a stairwell that turned

Painters Karen and Elaine avoiding plaster dust

out to be something of a jigsaw puzzle. Larry skill-fully built stairs, and his nephews, Jerry and Jeff, helped install a water heater. Bob helped the French electrician install lighting. Nathan and Stan worked on a new roof. Dave and Sean installed a shower. And Linda, Millie, and Connie made certain the team was well fed.

Some men from the three congregations came to help after their workday ended, staying long after the United States group, dirty and exhausted, de-parted for the night. Day after draining day the team labored midst a cloud of plaster dust.

As the week sped by, there seemed to be little time to share the gospel and witness. Plus, only one of the group spoke some French. (Sean was taking a high school French class.) "As we made neighborhood trips to buy groceries, launder clothes, and pick up delicious French pastries," Karen says, "we hoped our English would be understood. We explained to people what we were doing at the church and invited them to come and see for themselves."

On Sunday the team joined with two of the congregations for worship. At the French Caribbean service, the people greeted their American guests warmly. There were lots of wide, wonderful smiles. Sometimes the welcome was expressed in halting English; often it was a cordial "bonjour."

"These people were different than the ones we saw on the Metro," Karen comments. "There was a sparkle in their eyes and a genuine feeling of camaraderie. As the service began, we sang along the best we could. The words were projected on a screen, but there was just enough repetition that I found myself singing in French as well."

The congregation prepared to take Communion. "Thousands of miles from home among people whose language we did not understand," Karen says, "we shared the bread and cup. And though we spoke different languages and our outward appearances were different, our hearts were united in remembrance of what Christ had done for all of us."

The same atmosphere prevailed in the Arabic-speaking service in the afternoon. The Americans were impressed with the congregation's vitality and found the music uplifting. "Even though we had no idea what the words meant," Karen says, "the message was clear."

The team sharing in a Sunday worship service

Pastor Noel, a retired pastor from First Church, filled in for Pastor Farag, who was filling in for Trevor at the Versailles Church. Noel preached in French, Trevor interpreted into English, and another person interpreted into Arabic for the rest of the group. "None of them missed a beat," Karen says. "Each spoke with passion, and I was amazed at how smoothly it went and marveled at the different languages. Love in every language was certainly spoken there that morning."

The Work and Witness team members spent a few evenings with some of the local pastors, listening to their testimonies and hearing their concerns for the people of France. "What a difficult task they have," Karen says. "In this country it's not considered 'proper' to speak of your faith or religion. Not only is it improper, but individuals can lose their jobs if they witness at work, and they may be detained if they try to evangelize on the street. The French consider religion a private matter and want to keep it that way."

Karen realized she was *witnessed to* more than she *witnessed*.

Pastor Martinez, associate pastor in Versailles, talked about the slow growth of the church. He mentioned that evangelizing is extremely difficult and the Nazarene Church is still considered a cult in France. "But each time I walk into my church and see the people there," Rev. Martinez said, "I praise God for the miracles. Each of them is a miracle."

The team finished as much work as they could in their allotted time. "But I realized that the work is never done," Karen says. "Even though the building will one day be completed, the real work of bringing souls to Christ will continue and be incomplete until His return."

Before leaving France, Karen reflected on her previous ponderings. *Would I be a witness?* she had wondered. *Would I really have the opportunity to share the gospel?*

Now, as she reflected upon her days in Paris, Karen realized she was *witnessed to* more than she *witnessed*. "We worshiped with our brothers and sisters in Christ," she says. "And we shared Christ with the people in the community the best we could, despite a language barrier, by our smiles and love for the people.

Karen (left) with her husband, Bob, and Elaine, relaxing at a Paris sidewalk café

"But as I thought about the people of France—people I had perceived to have a Christian heritage—I realized how little I had known about them. The few who openly talk about their faith encounter persecution in both subtle and not-so-subtle ways. I found it difficult to accept the fact that people can lose their jobs just for testifying for Jesus Christ or that my church is considered a cult. And when I considered the devotion of Trevor Johnston, Noel, Farag, Rev. Martinez, and the dedicated Nazarene laypeople I met, I realized I had truly been *witnessed to*. The French people and this Work and Witness trip have made a tremendous impact on my life!"

A $1,650 Bargain

"Here, Cesar, catch!" Ed hollered as he tossed up the man's shoe to him. The slim Filipino, standing on a narrow plank beside the partially finished concrete-block wall, grabbed it with one hand, placed it on his bare foot, and scampered across the wooden scaffolding with the agility of a bobcat. Clad in T-shirt, khaki shorts, and well-worn sandals, he returned to his job, pouring a concrete support beam. I, Wes Eby, stared with fascination as this craftsman helped finish the work I was supposed to do.

Watching Cesar, I backed away from the building and plopped under a banana tree. The 105-degree weather had sapped my energy. A writer and editor by profession, I lacked both physical and mental preparedness for manual labor in Manila's unexpected heat and humidity. Nearing the end of my 10-day stay in the Philippines, I was exhausted—totally.

Our 11-member Work and Witness team had flown to the Philippines to help build a combination church-parsonage. Along with the construction project, we would assist with Sunday services and a few weeknight evangelistic meetings. The group was comprised of 2 husband-wife couples (Ray and Marlene Kelley, Joe and Carolyn Carr), a family of 3

(Marty, Ruth, and Ryan Butler), and 2 father-son duos (Dan and Kent Funkhouser, Wes and Ed Eby).

The Overland Park Church of the Nazarene, located in a Kansas City suburb, had planned this venture for a year and a half. We had strategized and promoted and prayed. The congregation committed $20,000—indeed, a miracle—for the purchase of building materials. We raised money in any way we could. One simple method was to enlist church members to become "ADADs," which stood for a-dime-a-day givers. Over a period of 16 months, the donors—which included teens, young adults, baby boomers, and prime-timers—contributed $50 each,

The "teamsters"

and many ADADs equaled hundreds of dollars.

Support came from unexpected sources. Family members, friends, and church folks donated tools and supplies, which we planned to leave in the Philippines. One woman even made carpenters' aprons for the entire team. And, of course, the "teamsters"—as I affectionately dubbed them—each agreed to raise $1,650 for their own expenses.

Their smiles cracked the crust of fatigue that encased us.

"Why are you spending all that money going to the Philippines?" we heard more than once. One well-meaning critic muttered, "Goodness, the amount for 11 people is more than $18,000. Why don't you just send the cash instead? Just think what good it could do." Our feeble attempts to explain why we were going never seemed to satisfy the few nonsupporters. Undeterred, we forged ahead with our plans.

After months of anticipation, we packed our suitcases, tying neon-orange ribbon to the handles for easy identification in airports. We checked in at the Kansas City International Airport, including 21 pieces of luggage, with no problems. We hugged our loved ones, said our good-byes, grabbed our carry-ons, and boarded the Northwest Airlines 747 jumbo jet for our 20-hour flight via Los Angeles and Tokyo. Since the sun didn't set until we were near Manila, this seemed like the longest day of my life.

Arriving on a Saturday night, we were most thankful that the following day was Sunday. We needed it. And we hadn't even worked a lick yet.

Wes taking a turn at hauling concrete

The Filipinos welcomed us graciously and warmly. Their smiles cracked the crust of fatigue that encased us, and we were soon caught up in the freedom and joy of their worship. The Sabbath truly was a day of rest.

Work started early on Monday. And hard labor it was. As we dug footers with shovels and picks, we would have paid any amount to rent a backhoe. As we sifted sand using a handmade sieve, we wondered where the nearest Home Depot was located. As we hauled buckets of concrete up to the second floor by rope and pulley and poured concrete floors in the parsonage using wheelbarrows, how we longed for a cement truck.

But what rewarding labor! Each afternoon we left the work site, energy depleted, but gratified at all that had been accomplished. The reason? The people. Yes, our brothers and sisters in the Philippines.

Pastor Ronny Cruz and his wife, Reyzie, labored with us every day—he in construction and she in the kitchen. Young men—Jun Jun, Rinaldo, Nick, Marlin, J. C., and Isaac—faithfully came to help in countless ways. Ignacio and his crew completed tasks we could never have done. Nene, Nilda, Miding, Irma, Armida, and Maribel assisted Reyzie in feeding the teamsters and the entire work crew with hot lunches.

Tears cut through the grime on my cheeks; the sleeve of my sweaty T-shirt became a Kleenex.

The man we came to know as Cesar met us when we arrived each morning around 7. He worked beside us, matching and even surpassing our efforts, certainly mine. After a couple of days, we learned that Cesar was a night watchman. In the late afternoon when we left the church, he cleaned up, snatched a two-hour nap, and went to his full-time job. The next morning, often without any more sleep, he was always there to greet us. And this daily pattern continued day after scorching day.

Cesar's wife, Nilda, also held a daytime job. Even though she could not help the teamsters all the time, she worked with us whenever possible.

We also learned that Cesar and his family lived in a lean-to adjacent to the church. Their one-room, dirt-floor home had no inside plumbing. Nor was there a front door; they simply pulled a large sheet of plywood across the front each night for privacy.

On Friday of the first week, a missionary told us that one of Cesar's children had been bitten by a rat

Cesar in front of his home

during the night. After taking his daughter to the doctor, the girl was given a series of injections for rabies.

As I observed Cesar that memorable day near the conclusion of our work, my vision blurred. Tears cut through the grime on my cheeks; the sleeve of my sweaty T-shirt became a Kleenex. His lifestyle, so different from mine, made me seem like a millionaire. Indeed, by "worldly" standards of my home country, I was wealthy. Yet, as I considered his commitment, his sacrifices, his poverty, I knew he was the one who was *rich* and I was the one who was *poor.* It was then I realized how naive I had been about missions. It was then I truly understood why I had spent the money to travel to the Philippines.

I was raised in a Nazarene minister's home by mission-minded parents. I grew up, surrounded by missionary kinfolks. A favorite aunt, my step-mom, my youngest brother, and four cousins were serving—or would serve—on the mission field. I had heard their stories, had seen their pictures, and had discussed their experiences with them. I believed I was missions-aware, that I knew what the mission field was like. I even possessed an unholy pride about my mission heritage.

The Lord used Cesar to impact me, to speak to me in a fresh way, to "preach" a message I needed. I was changed. Comprehension of Christ's command "to go" gripped me as never before. This new understanding would never have happened if I had stayed at home in Kansas. This revelation—this miracle—came on a Work and Witness trip, because I chose "to go."

Work and Witness proved to me that the vicarious can never substitute for the real. I had to see for myself the challenges missionaries, national pastors, and layleaders confront in working for the Lord in other world areas. In the Philippines, I obtained a greater appreciation for the personal sacrifices our missionaries make, and there I encountered "rich" Cesar, a special layman. For me, the $1,650 trip to Manila put an indelible face on missions that reminds me to intercede faithfully and give sacrificially on behalf of those represented by that face.

Just see what $1,650 bought. What a bargain!